VIOLENCE AND SOCIETY™

VIOLENCE IN MOVIES, MUSIC, AND THE MEDIA

JEANNE NAGLE

Rosen PUBLISHING®

New York

To Chris

Published in 2009 by The Rosen Publishing Group, Inc.
29 East 21st Street, New York, NY 10010

Library of Congress Cataloging-in-Publication Data

Nagle, Jeanne M.
Violence in music, movies, and the media / Jeanne Nagle—1st ed.
    p. cm.—(Violence and society)
Includes bibliographical references and index.
ISBN-13: 978-1-4042-1795-9 (library binding)
1. Violence in mass media. I. Title.
P95.V5N34 2009
303.6—dc22

2007050913

Manufactured in Malaysia

On the cover: Left: Johnny Knoxville and Dwayne "The Rock" Johnson in a promotional poster for the 2003 movie *Walking Tall*. Right: Rapper 50 Cent.

CONTENTS

INTRODUCTION

Violence is a part of entertainment in our society. For example, the popular television show *The Sopranos* *(above)* regularly featured murder and mayhem.

L ook back to just about any era in history and you'll find plenty of violent events that have passed for entertainment. The Coliseum in ancient Rome had seating for tens of thousands to watch gladiators fight to the death. In the sixteenth and seventeenth centuries, public punishment such as being put in the stocks or being "dunked" as a witch delighted spectators. Large crowds regularly turned out to witness executions, from crucifixions in ancient Rome to beheadings in revolutionary France to hangings in the old American West.

These days, violent entertainment comes in different forms. If you listen to the radio, watch television or movies, play video games, or surf the Internet, you'll notice that violence is one of the ways that we entertain ourselves. For example, plenty of music lyrics describe anger, fighting, and hostility. Similarly, abuse, murder, gunfights, and explosions are common in popular films and television shows. Many of the best-selling video games encourage participants to hunt or kill opponents. And it has become all too easy to download videos from the Internet showing beatings and street fights, among other acts of violence.

The precise effects of violent music, movies, and media are not easy to determine, especially when it comes to children and adolescents. Beginning in the 1950s, many studies have been conducted in this area. Researchers have found correlations, or connections, between violence in entertainment and real-world

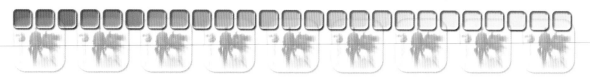

hostility. But no one has been able to prove conclusively that the violence we see and hear can cause us to become violent. Despite this lack of hard evidence, it's likely that we are negatively influenced by the violent messages and situations that we encounter through the entertainment media.

Why is media violence so prevalent? How does media violence influence us? What are people doing to try to change our violent entertainment media? These are just a few of the important questions answered in this book.

I t seems that whenever a source of entertainment starts to become popular, someone raises concerns about the negative effect it might have on children. Throughout history, this has been the case with movies, various genres of music, and television. Today, the same concerns arise regarding the Internet and video games. These media have come under scrutiny soon after their arrival on the cultural landscape. One issue in particular has concerned parents, politicians, teachers, law enforcement officials, and doctors. That issue is violent content in entertainment media.

Of course, what one person sees as violent another might see as harmless fun. So, what exactly is violence? Why do people get so upset about violence in the entertainment media? And how did this debate begin?

Violence and Its Role in Entertainment

Violence is any forceful action that is meant to cause harm. There are two basic forms of violence: physical and emotional. Physical violence causes injury to a person's body or some-one's property. Emotional violence affects the mind, damaging an individual's sense of safety and well-being. When people hear the word "violence," they usually think of the physical kind. This is because the results of physical violence are easy to detect—cuts and bruises on a person's body, or damaged

Both physical and emotional violence are featured in horror movies like *Hostel*. Characters may be taunted and stalked before they are tortured or killed.

property. Emotional violence, on the other hand, injures the mind, so its effects are difficult to observe.

Both physical violence and emotional violence are widely represented in movies, music, television, and new media (the Internet and other forms of digital information). In entertainment media, the stronger focus seems to be on physical violence. Shootings, murder, explosions, and beatings are common themes. However, emotional violence is often depicted as well. Threats, blackmail, bullying, and stalking are all examples of emotional violence. Using hateful or discriminatory words also falls in this second category.

Real-world violence comes in different levels or degrees. Consider, for instance, the difference between a slap in the face and a grisly murder. The level of entertainment violence also varies. One movie may feature a single fistfight, while another is filled from beginning to end with blown-up buildings and bloodshed.

Representations of Violence

Not many would insist that all violence be taken out of movies, music, and television shows simply because it is unpleasant. Violence and conflict are a part of real life, so sometimes these elements need to be included in entertainment to tell a realistic story or share an honest point of view. When it comes to entertainment, the issue is not usually whether violence is involved but how it is presented.

There are several tricks of the trade that can make violent content either more horrifying or less offensive. Take special effects, for example. Back in the early days of television and

Special effects helped make the violent death of Sonny Corleone in *The Godfather* disturbing but memorable.

movies, when characters were shot, they would simply clutch their stomachs and fall to the ground. This is not the case anymore. Today's technology makes it possible to show all sorts of details—from gushing wounds to digitally enhanced fireballs— that make the violence more realistic. Studies show that more realistic violence has a stronger negative effect on audiences.

Sound effects and music also play a role in how violence is presented in the entertainment media. Just as visual special effects have gotten more realistic, so, too, have the soundtracks in movies, television, and video games. Gunshots ring and bones crunch loudly, enhancing the effect of the violence. Music, meanwhile, sets the mood for violent scenes. Certain rhythms build suspense, and loud, fast music can make people excited or afraid. Also, if happy, upbeat music is played during a violent scene, the audience may not be as repulsed by the violence as they normally would.

Questions About Cause and Effect

The current debate revolves around how people are affected by exposure to violent content in the entertainment media. Many scientists, doctors, politicians, and parents believe there is a strong connection between entertainment violence and aggressive behavior. Aggression is a forceful action intended to dominate or hurt someone. These folks say that people who spend a lot of time watching or listening to violent content get used to it and come to think that it's OK to act aggressively.

Young children are considered to be the most at risk of becoming aggressive after seeing or hearing violent entertainment. The theory is that because they are still learning the difference

With every click of the remote control, young viewers risk coming face-to-face with violent images on television.

between make-believe and reality, they have a harder time separating the two. Therefore, children may think that violence is a normal, acceptable way to solve problems.

People defending the entertainment industry say it's not fair to blame movies, music, television, and new media for aggressive behavior in young people. After all, these are not the only sources of violence in this world. Still others suggest that only people who are aggressive to begin with react badly to violence in entertainment.

Movies Start Off with a Bang

The very first images captured on film, in the late 1800s, showed a few moments of common events such as people performing acrobatics or sneezing. People watched these moving pictures alone in small booths using a specially designed eyepiece that acted like a magnifying glass. There was nothing violent about these images.

That changed in 1895 with the arrival of *Mary Queen of Scots*, a movie that employed what is considered the first special effect. Using a dummy and tricky camera work, the film's producers showed a beheading—complete with the executioner displaying the disembodied head for all to see. *The Great Train Robbery* (1903), which is considered the first commercial film, was also violent. Supposedly based on real-life holdups by members of Butch Cassidy's famous Hole in the Wall gang, the movie featured the beating of a clerk, two cold-blooded murders, robbery of passengers at gunpoint, and a shootout that ends in several deaths. Incredibly, all of this was packed into just twelve minutes of running time!

The Great Train Robbery (1903) was filled with violent acts. Here, in a still from the film, a gunman takes direct aim at the audience.

Objections to such movie violence started early. In 1908, the Chicago police department refused a permit for theaters to screen *The James Boys in Missouri* and *Night Riders*. Authorities claimed the movies celebrated violence and would lead viewers to commit crimes. The result was *Block v. Chicago*, the first legal case in the United States to consider violence in the movies. The Illinois Supreme Court ruled in favor of the police department. It ruled that the films were "immoral, and their exhibition would necessarily be attended with evil effects on youthful spectators."

The year 1929 marked the start of scientific investigation into movie violence. The Payne Fund Studies were a series of investigations into how movies affected the way children learned, felt, and behaved. Researchers found that children remembered movie scenes that contained crime and fighting more readily than other, less violent scenes. The studies also showed that movies influence kids at play to imitate characters and reenact scenes.

History of Violence in Music

Violent lyrics in music are nothing new. Songs called ballads have been popular in many countries since ancient times. In medieval England, for instance, traveling singers called minstrels performed ballads that were basically musical news reports. Typical topics of ballads were battles being fought in distant locations, or the acts of a particularly mighty warrior. Minstrels also entertained the king and his subjects with musical tales of outlaws, both real and imagined, who roamed the countryside.

A similar tradition could be found in Mexican culture in the 1800s. Upbeat ballads known as *corridos* told stories of violent bandits and barroom fights. At first, a lot of these songs came from

the singers' imaginations. Eventually, though, they started to describe actual events from the singers' lives. Corridos describing disputes along the Mexico–Texas border became especially popular. They celebrated the real-life brave men who fought—and sometimes killed—the Anglos (white Americans) who were trying to take their land.

Rappers like 50 Cent say their lyrics simply describe life as they experience it. However, critics say some types of rap music are unnecessarily violent.

It wasn't until a century later, in the mid-1980s, that people really started to take organized action against violent content in music. At that time, rap hit the airwaves. Concerns had been raised about the violent and sexual content of many punk, rock, and heavy metal songs, but rap took even more heat. Starting in the 1990s, numerous studies attempted to determine the potential harm done by exposure to rap lyrics. Controversy over rap and violence continues unabated to this day.

Violence and the Tube

Television sets have been around since 1932, but regular programming didn't begin until almost ten years later. Even then, there weren't many shows on the air. However, after World War II, the four American networks—NBC, CBS, ABC, and the Dumont Television Network—offered a lot more programs. By 1951, these included twenty-seven hours of children's shows.

Early shows were geared toward a middle-class family audience. They were wholesome programs designed to entertain, not offend, the average American. Action-adventure shows were popular, including crime dramas such as *Martin Kane: Private Eye*, police shows such as *Dragnet*, and westerns for kids (*Hopalong Cassidy*) and adults (*Death Valley Days*).

The violence in these shows was tame, especially when compared to what the average viewer sees nowadays. However, it was enough to upset certain groups, namely the National Catholic Conference on Family Life and the Southern California Association for Better Radio and Television. Their protestations caught the attention of the Federal Communications Commission (FCC), the U.S. government agency formed in 1934 to oversee

Over the years, numerous congressional hearings have been held to address violent content in music, movies, and the media. In 1999, Senators Orrin Hatch *(left)* and Joe Lieberman added their voices to the debate.

radio and television broadcasting. Before long, the U.S. Congress began a series of hearings on the matter. (Congressional hearings help the federal government analyze a situation to decide whether it should take action by creating or enforcing laws.) Three hearings—in 1952, 1954, and 1955—were just the beginning of many investigations into violence on television.

Inappropriate Content on the Web

The technology behind the Internet was developed in the late 1950s. However, it wasn't until 1991 that the World Wide Web was made public. Suddenly, anyone with a modem and inexpensive software could post pages on the Internet. This was both good and bad. It was good in that it provided the public with a tremendous amount of information from various sources. However, it was bad because broad public access meant that the Web was difficult to regulate. Without strong regulation, the Web came to contain a lot of violent information and images that were offensive to a great many people.

Before long, parties were trying to find ways to shield children and young adults from violent content on the Internet. In a statement before the U.S. Senate Judiciary Committee in 1999, Utah senator Orrin Hatch recommended filtering. This technology involves using special software to block the transmission of offensive Web content on school computers. Motivated by Hatch's speech, the Senate wrote the Children's Internet Protection Act, which was signed into law in December 2000. Much more research and legislation on this topic is expected.

The Rise of Violent Video Games

In the 1950s, the only place you could play electronic games was in a university computer lab. That's because the first games were designed to run on either a large mainframe computer or sophisticated electronic test equipment. The games themselves were very simple. Many of them were based on nonviolent games already in existence, such as tic-tac-toe and tennis.

By the early 1970s, games could be played on a television set at home, or on consoles in arcades. The Magnavox Odyssey game system for home use arrived in 1972. It was quickly overtaken by the Atari game system. Atari's now-famous *PONG* game, adapted from a version that was played in video arcades, was a huge seller in 1975.

Only one year later, people were voicing concern over the presence of violence in video games. An arcade game called *Death Race*, for example, had video-car drivers running over human-like "gremlins" to score points. The game outraged parents and government officials alike. The U.S. National Safety Council labeled the game "sick and morbid." Magazines and television news shows, including CBS's *60 Minutes*, ran stories on *Death Race* and the effect that violent video games might have on young minds. The game also inspired the first organized protest against video game violence.

CHAPTER TWO
A Closer Look at Violent Entertainment

On the surface, movies, music, and television offer up harmless and glamorous entertainment. The Hollywood directors and actors, television stars, and recording artists whom we admire wouldn't set out to harm us. Plus, lots of people play video games and surf the Web all the time, and most of those people are perfectly normal. These statements are basically true. But if you look closely at our entertainment media, you will find that each one contains an element of violence—although this is not necessarily the same as promoting violence. This chapter highlights the historical debates around the issue of media violence.

Movie Violence and the Hays Code

In the early days of cinema, film producers came under attack by groups claiming that movies had a negative influence on children. In response, movie producers and distributors created the Motion Picture Production Code, or Hays Code, in 1930. The code was a list of rules that producers created concerning what could and could not be shown onscreen. Behavior that was off-limits included murder, crime, and "repellent acts" such as brutality, gruesomeness, and cruelty to children or animals. Swearing and sex were also forbidden in the movies.

Many producers and directors essentially ignored the Hays Code, which was not strictly enforced. To keep them

As the bloody, gory battles of World War II took place in the real world, the Hays Code sought to keep violent scenes off Hollywood's big screen.

in line, the Motion Picture Producers and Distributors of America created the Production Code Administration in 1934. With stronger enforcement, the Hays Code largely succeeded in keeping violence and other offensive material out of Hollywood movies for years. Foreign films, however, were not covered by the rules that regulated Hollywood films, and, eventually, an imported film sparked a battle that brought about the end of the Hays Code.

In 1950, the New York State Board of Regents sought to ban theaters from showing the Italian film *The Miracle*. Officials claimed the movie was sacrilegious, or disrespectful of religious beliefs. The case went all the way to the U.S. Supreme Court, which ultimately ruled against the ban, in 1952. The ruling stated that movies were covered under the First Amendment, which guarantees the right to freedom of expression.

After the ruling, Hollywood moviemakers started including material that once had been prohibited, and by the mid-1960s, the Hays Code was abandoned. The Motion Picture Association of America (MPAA) rating system replaced it. This new system took into account what content was appropriate for viewers by age, instead of simply forbidding "unfit" material. Although it has undergone a few minor changes, this MPAA rating system has remained intact and is still in effect.

Violence and Music

Throughout the 1950s and 1960s, rock and roll had plenty of critics. But the concerns were less about violence and more about sex and drugs. The 1960s were a time of peace protests and the nonviolent civil rights movement, so a lot of music in that decade was about ending war and hatred. Violent lyrics wouldn't have made sense. However, one form of music that started in the 1960s—heavy metal—did make a point of using violent content. This macho, guitar-driven music often contained lyrics with dark, disturbing images. Later, in the 1970s, punk rock shocked and worried many adults. Punks rejected mainstream society, and rebellion was a huge part of the punk culture. In addition to commenting on social and political issues, the lyrics of punk songs were typically violent.

Slayer was one of the bands that concerned the Parents Music Resource Center when it came to the issue of offensive lyrics.

The Parents Music Resource Center

In 1985, the wives of five Washington politicians formed the Parents Music Resource Center (PMRC). The PMRC was designed to call attention to violent and sexual references in recordings and music videos. The group called for the Recording Industry Association of America (RIAA) to voluntarily put labels on

PARENTAL ADVISORY EXPLICIT LYRICS

The Parents Music Resource Center convinced the recording industry to stick this warning label on music with inappropriate and violent content.

recordings, similar to the MPAA rating system that is in place for movies.

The RIAA refused to label recordings for various reasons. They claimed it was unclear who would decide which recordings got labeled, and they argued that putting warnings on their product would cause sales to drop. In addition, they made the argument that the labeling system was a form of censorship that violated the right of free expression. (Read more about this issue in "The Censorship Argument" in chapter 3.)

In the summer of 1985, a congressional hearing pitted senators and members of the PMRC against the recording industry and several popular musicians of the day, including Dee Snider of the metal band Twisted Sister and rock musician Frank Zappa. The recording artists made it clear that they were strongly against labeling, but the RIAA eventually agreed to use the parental advisory system anyway.

Does Rap Get a Bad Rap?

The musical genre of rap has long been under intense scrutiny, in large part because so many young people listen to it. A 2005 study published in the *Journal of Adolescent Research* indicates that rap is the favorite music of young adults in grades seven through twelve, regardless of race or gender.

Throughout its history, rap has received much negative attention for its references to violence. Begun in the 1970s, rapping became a way for urban musicians to express their dissatisfaction with the poverty and crime they saw all around them. This self-expression took a violent turn in the 1980s with the arrival of gangsta rap, which many critics say glorified crime and hostility instead of raging against it. Of special concern has been gangsta rap's heavy use of lyrics that refer to violence against women and the police.

Rap artists say it is unfair to put all the blame on their music. They say that their lyrics simply hold up a mirror to the violent reality that they face every day. They further point out that other forms of music—country and folk, for example—have long

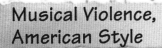

Musical Violence, American Style

Rappers' claims that other musical styles portray violence are certainly true. Here are just a few examples found in two American musical art forms, country and the blues.

- "Banks of the Ohio"—One of the first country songs ever recorded (in 1928), it describes a man murdering his girlfriend and tossing her body in the river.

- "Sam Hill"—This song has a murderer lashing out before being hanged. Many artists have recorded the song, including singer and actor Tex Ritter (on his 1935 album *Blood on the Saddle*) and country music legend Johnny Cash.

- "Folsom Prison Blues"— Cash wrote and recorded this song of a man who's in prison because he shot another man "just to watch him die." This song, in addition to other similar tunes, led MTV to dub Cash the "Original Gangsta" in 2003.

- "She Stabbed Me with an Ice Pick" and "Terrible Murder Blues"—The titles of these blues songs say it all.

Johnny Cash performs for inmates at Folsom Prison, in Folsom, California, in 1968.

histories of describing violence. But you never hear about anyone in Nashville being accused of causing crime rates to soar.

Music Videos

The violence-in-music discussion took on an added dimension when music videos came along. As the folks at MTV quickly discovered in 1981, images and music together are a potent combination. Adding visuals to music gave recording artists an additional way to get their message across. With videos, viewers didn't have to picture in their minds what the words meant—the artists showed them, often graphically. Below are a few examples of videos from different musical genres that have faced opposition.

- **NWA, "Alwayz Into Somethin'" (1991).** This video features gunfire and violent crime from beginning to end, including NWA rappers shooting into the camera.
- **Beastie Boys, "Body Movin'" (1998).** Censored and uncensored versions were released; the "nicer" version showed gunfire from lasers instead of machine guns.
- **Madonna, "What It Feels Like for a Girl" (2000).** Basically a nonstop series of violent acts, this video includes deliberate car crashes, gunplay, violent crime, and suicide. MTV and VH1 each aired it once and then banned it.
- **50 Cent, "I'll Still Kill" (2007).** Originally renamed "I Still Will" by the artist's own record company, the video has been banned from MTV and Black Entertainment Television (BET).

A Legacy of Television Violence

The first major report investigating the effect of television on children came out in 1961. Called "Television in the Lives of Our Children," it was based on the results of twenty-one studies conducted throughout the United States and Canada during the previous three years. The report stated that television content was "extremely violent." Researchers concluded not only that television was violent, but that television violence could contribute to delinquent behavior in children.

The Networks Have Their Say

Since that first report, television and its effect on children have been the subject of many more studies. In light of the reports that criticized violent television programs, the major television networks finally decided to conduct studies of their own. ABC's "Studies in Violence and Television" (1976) and CBS's "Television Violence and the Adolescent Boy" (1978) both concluded that violent television content did indeed have a negative effect on teenagers—at least on teenage boys. NBC's "Television and Aggression" (1982), on the other hand, reported that television violence had no effect whatsoever on children. It was later discovered, however, that three out of the four researchers involved were NBC employees, so their report couldn't be trusted.

Joining Forces

In the 1990s, the networks worked together to create voluntary guidelines on violent programming. These were designed to cut

back on gratuitous (purposeless) and excessive violence, and limit scenes depicting the use of force or torture, including animal abuse. The agreement also forbade the use of realistic violence in children's programs.

The networks' agreement led to the creation of parental advisories in 1993. These warnings are seen onscreen at the beginning of most programs. Similar to the ratings found on

Onscreen advisory tags let parents know which television programs their children can watch without being exposed to violence or sexual content.

movies and music recordings, the advisories let viewers know if a show contains nudity, violence, sexual content, or inappropriate language. In 1994, the National Cable Television Association followed the networks' lead and put in place parental advisories and a violence rating system for cable television programs.

Television Violence Today

The grassroots organization Parents Television Council announced that the 2006–2007 television season was the most violent one ever. This news again stirred up discussions about violence in television programming—discussions that have never really gone away since the 1950s.

In April 2007, the Federal Communications Commission (FCC) issued a report titled "Violent Television Programming and Its Impact on Children." This report concluded that the U.S. government should fully regulate what is shown on television. That would mean giving the FCC more power over network television programming and control over basic cable content, which it never had before.

The FCC report sparked interest in television violence on Capitol Hill and resulted in another congressional hearing a few months later. Led by West Virginia senator Jay Rockefeller, the hearing basically echoed concerns stated in the FCC report and urged Congress to take charge of television programming. Network and cable executives say the report and the hearing will have little to no impact on broadcasting, as the FCC's proposals would violate their constitutional right to freedom of expression. Undaunted, Senator Rockefeller began drafting legislation that would seek to regulate and curb television violence.

Within two years of being posted on YouTube (www.youtube.com), this clip of street fights had been viewed by more than three million people.

Violence and the Web

A couple of unique factors have put the Internet in a league of its own when it comes to violent entertainment media. First, the Web hasn't been around as long as most other media, so there isn't much scientific research into the long-term effects of Internet violence. Second, because it is essentially an open forum that belongs to everyone, the Internet has been spared the same

kind of rules and restrictions that have been placed on other entertainment media.

That's not to say there is no violence on the Web, however. At the click of a mouse, surfers can find violent content, including commercial music videos, how-to videos for making bombs, and violent online games. Many sites specialize in posting exactly the kinds of gross, gory, and violent material that gets banned from other media.

Kids and teens from all over the world flock to these kinds of sites. A 2005 Media Awareness Network survey revealed that more than one-third of Canadian boys in grades seven to eleven have visited at least one site featuring primarily violent content. They didn't just stumble across this material, either. They went there on purpose, to experience the violence.

Violence and Video Games

Because games are competitions, it makes sense that people who play them might get a little aggressive in order to win. When aggression gets out of control, however, the game may turn violent, with opponents trying to hurt each other, not just win.

With most video games currently on the market, violence is not something to avoid. It is the object of the game. Violent video games have been around almost from the start. Released in 1978, the arcade game *Space Invaders* had players shooting at aliens as they dropped from the stars. In 1980, Atari's *Battlezone* had gamers blowing up simulated tanks. The action was so realistic that a version of the game was created for use by the U.S. Army.

Games got more realistic in the 1990s, thanks to technology breakthroughs such as graphics accelerators. The 1990s also saw the arrival of interactivity, which allowed players to feel more

The realistic, and some say senseless, violence of video games such as *Grand Theft Auto* frequently gets the attention of politicians and media watchdog groups.

like they were actually inside the game instead of just playing it. In 1994, the gaming industry created the Entertainment Software Rating Board (ESRB), which rates games and enforces self-regulated guidelines. *Doom*—which featured 3-D graphics, first-person shooters, and multiple-player capability—was the first video game to receive a "Mature" rating from the ESRB.

The release of *Grand Theft Auto* in 1998 marked a violent change in the way video games were played. Instead of bravely

fighting cartoon aliens, players stole and killed to become crime lords and win game points.

The Government Weighs In

Concern over the violent content of video games led to the U.S. Juvenile Justice Act in 1999. This policy statement, issued by the Senate Judiciary Committee, encourages corporations to make responsible decisions concerning media violence and its availability to children. In addition, the U.S. Trade Commission released a report in 2000 detailing how corporations were marketing violent video games specifically to young children. But the reports didn't faze industry executives, who continued to make their games more interactive and realistic. In 2002, *Grand Theft Auto 3* caused a major uproar with its even more realistic graphics and gratuitous violence. Such games continue to be produced and bought in huge numbers, with the violence getting kicked up a notch with each new title.

CHAPTER THREE

Issues Surrounding Violent Entertainment

The American Academy of Pediatrics estimates that more than 3,500 studies have been conducted on entertainment media violence and its effects on children. These studies have covered violence in movies, music, television, video games, and the Internet from many different angles, reaching wide-ranging conclusions. The results of these studies have brought into focus several key issues.

Like the Real Thing

"Realism" describes a style of portraying made-up events in a way that is as close to genuine as possible. Realism lets people feel as though they are having new, sometimes thrilling, experiences from the safety of their own homes or the movie theater. The problem is that young children often can't tell what is real and what is make-believe to begin with, let alone fantasy that is made to look as real as possible. Take, for instance, the 1999 case of a seven-year-old boy in Dallas, Texas. He accidentally killed his three-year-old brother while imitating a "clothesline" move he saw on a World Wrestling Federation match on television.

Violence and Body Chemistry

It is difficult, if not impossible, to determine the exact effect of violence on the mind. However, science has proven that

Playing video games will continue to be a pastime for children in the foreseeable future. Nobody knows for sure what long-term effects video violence will have on young minds.

being exposed to media violence has a measurable effect on the body. Violent content in entertainment media gets the heart beating rapidly, the blood flowing faster, and the lungs pumping quicker. This is the same bodily reaction that occurs when we are faced with danger in the real world, through what is known as the body's "fight-or-flight" response. Our bodies release chemicals, like adrenaline and cortisol, in preparation for either running away or staying and fighting. When we sense violence in our

environment, our bodies do not fully differentiate between fantasy and reality. They just react the way they're genetically programmed to when facing a threat. Sensory impressions intensify, sight sharpens, impulses quicken, and the perception of pain diminishes. These are powerful physiological reactions.

Recent research indicates that people can actually become addicted to violent media. When we are entertained, our brains release dopamine, a chemical that makes us feel pleasure. Dopamine is the same brain chemical that makes people feel happy when they take drugs. Experiments conducted in 1998 at London's Hammersmith Hospital showed that the level of dopamine doubled in the brains of kids playing video games. That's similar to the effects of getting a shot of the heavy-duty stimulant amphetamine.

If we entertain ourselves with violent media, our brains may associate exposure to violence with feeling good. When it is exposed to dopamine, the brain naturally wants more—a craving known as addiction.

Habituation and Desensitization

When researchers study the effect of media violence on children and teenagers, they look for two particular reactions. One is habituation, which occurs when people get so used to seeing and hearing violence that it doesn't bother them anymore. The other is desensitization, which occurs when people take in so much media violence that they become indifferent to all violence. In other words, watching and listening to violent content can permanently change the way children feel about and react to actual violence.

Frequent exposure to violent entertainment may make young children believe that violence is an acceptable way to resolve conflicts.

Scientists have known about desensitization for years. A study conducted by the National Institutes of Mental Health in 1982 determined that after seeing violence on television, children were more likely to be insensitive to the pain of others. More recently, in 2004, a study conducted at the University of Toledo determined that viewing violent movies and playing violent video games made grade school students less empathetic to, or

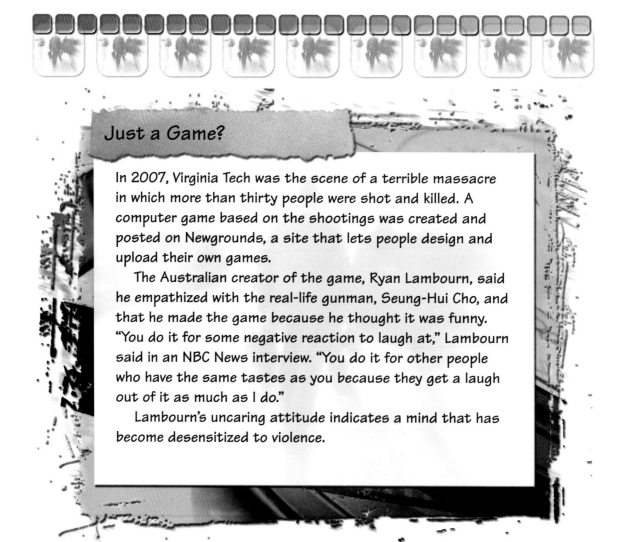

Just a Game?

In 2007, Virginia Tech was the scene of a terrible massacre in which more than thirty people were shot and killed. A computer game based on the shootings was created and posted on Newgrounds, a site that lets people design and upload their own games.

The Australian creator of the game, Ryan Lambourn, said he empathized with the real-life gunman, Seung-Hui Cho, and that he made the game because he thought it was funny. "You do it for some negative reaction to laugh at," Lambourn said in an NBC News interview. "You do it for other people who have the same tastes as you because they get a laugh out of it as much as I do."

Lambourn's uncaring attitude indicates a mind that has become desensitized to violence.

concerned about, people in the real world who were the victims of violence.

Media Violence and Gender Differences

Studies have shown that kids of all ages, races, classes, and family backgrounds are influenced by violent content in pretty much the same way. Boys, however, are more likely than girls

to encounter and be affected by entertainment violence. The majority of violent content, particularly on television, is geared toward male consumers, from storylines to interactive, first-person characters.

Young boys consume more media than young girls—about twenty-one minutes more each day. Researchers say that young boys watch more television and play more video games than girls, and that makes up the difference. Which medium boys prefer also varies from what girls like. Boys, especially when young, prefer violent and edgy television and gross-out movies. Girls listen to more music.

As for video games, boys prefer games with sports and action violence. Girls prefer fantasy violence, which involves scenes and stories that supposedly could in no way be thought of as real. The *Legend of Zelda* and *Final Fantasy X* are two titles considered fantasy games that contain violence.

Boys are more likely than girls to show aggression soon after being exposed to media violence. They are also more prone to overt acts of hostility or committing crimes, whereas females affected by media violence engage in indirect forms such as verbal abuse. The effect of exposure to media violence is longer-lasting on boys, too. Researchers found that boys who played violent video games were more likely than girls to show aggressive behavior later in life.

Girls and Violence in the Media

For a long time, scientists thought that no matter the circumstances, females just weren't aggressive. Consequently, up until the mid-1980s, there was very little research on female aggression.

That changed once entertainment executives realized there was a whole market out there that wasn't being targeted for sales. These executives paid attention to surveys that showed what kind of entertainment girls liked, and they started producing products that were aimed at them. For instance, one study showed that aggression increased in women aged eighteen to twenty-two when they were able to play violent video games with a female avatar. Despite some changes in the industry, young women still are typically shown as the victims of violence and not the heroes, especially in music and the movies. Rap and metal are full of lyrics about abusing women sexually or physically. In a 1995 study, researchers found that exposure to violent rap music led to greater acceptance of violence against women. Another study, published in 1998, showed that about one-quarter of the most popular video games of the time contained violent content in which women were victims.

Crime and Violent Entertainment

As mentioned in chapters 1 and 2, violent scenes in movies and on television have long been blamed for rising rates in juvenile crime. Nevertheless, a conclusive link between media violence and delinquency has never been established. In fact, fans of violent media point out that crime rates in the United States have been going down in recent years, even as the media allegedly get more violent.

Historically, many legal suits have been brought against entertainment media. These suits have attempted to make the media culpable (to blame) for influencing others' criminal behavior. Among the court cases are:

- *Olivia N. v. National Broadcasting Co.* (1974). The prosecution sued NBC because the rape of a nine-year-old girl was very similar to an assault shown in the television movie *Born Innocent*, which the girl's attackers had watched on NBC.

- *Zamora v. CBS* (1977). On trial for murdering his neighbor, fifteen-year-old Ronnie Zamora claimed "television intoxication," meaning that watching television had made him temporarily insane.

- *Waller v. Osbourne* (1991). Ozzy Osbourne was sued after it was claimed a young man committed suicide after repeatedly listening to the song "Suicide Solution." The same song was previously claimed as a factor in *McCollum v. CBS, Inc.* (1988).

- *Davidson v. Time Warner, Inc.* (1993). The family of a slain Texas trooper sued Tupac Shakur's record label after the killer, Ronald Ray Howard, said he was influenced by the rapper's anti-police lyrics; Howard was listening to Tupac's "Soulja's Story" at the time of the shooting.

Finnish teen Pekka-Eric Auvinen shot and killed seven students at his high school. Hours before the massacre, Auvinen posted a video on YouTube (*above*), using the dark and violent KMFDM song "Stray Bullet" as a soundtrack.

Because of the violent nature of Marilyn Manson's lyrics, city governments and media outlets worldwide have tried to censor his music.

The Censorship Argument

The First Amendment of the U.S. Constitution guarantees Americans' right to free speech. That means it is illegal for the government to make laws that prohibit people from expressing themselves. To do so is censorship.

Many believe censorship is a tool that the government should be able to use to guarantee public safety and well-being. But how do we determine what's harmful? Who gets to make that decision? These are questions at the heart of the debate over entertainment media violence.

The government, responding to public concerns about the effects of media violence on children and society, tries to find ways to lessen the amount of violence. The creators of media messages, on the other hand, claim the government is trampling their constitutional rights. They also question the value of limiting media violence. Keep in mind that despite all the studies, not one of them has proven beyond a doubt that media violence harms children. As long as these issues remain unclear, expect the entertainment media to continue to claim First Amendment protections when it comes to violent content.

CHAPTER FOUR
What Can Be Done?

W hen it comes to violence in movies, music, and the media, there is a difference of opinion over how the situation can be improved. Child psychologists and public safety advocates recommend strong measures to rein in the media. The marketplace, however, has its own ideas. Rarely do the two sides agree.

Self-Regulation

The entertainment media have not been forced by the government to eliminate violent content. However, they do need to respond to the concerns of the public so they won't lose the very consumers that make them profitable. To show that they take public concerns seriously, the entertainment industries vow to "clean up their own houses" through self-regulation.

Media self-regulation often involves some kind of ratings system, usually broken down by age. Movies have a ratings system that runs from G for "General Audiences" to NC-17, meaning that no one under the age of seventeen is allowed into the theater showing the film. Video games have E for "Everyone," T for "Teen," M for "Mature" (meaning age seventeen and older), and A for "Adults Only."

Television ratings also break down by age, labeling programs from TV-Y (suitable for viewers of all ages) through TV-MA (for mature audiences only). In addition, television

Advisory warnings are the entertainment industry's primary way of dealing with consumer objections to violent content.

advisories include a letter warning about questionable content: D for "Dialog," L for "Language" (swearing or sexual references), S for "Sex" or sexual situations, and V for "Violence."

Music recordings are simply labeled with the general warning "Parental Advisory: Explicit Content." This sticker covers everything from profanity and violent lyrics, to sexual content and references to drug use.

Are Ratings Effective?

Entertainment media ratings systems are useful as a guideline, but only when they are accurate. Because the systems are self-regulated, there is suspicion that violent content slips through under a rating that is lower than it should be. When the rating is lower, more people can enjoy different media, meaning that entertainment companies can make more money.

Movies provide a great example of the trouble with ratings. A study conducted in 2007 found that there has been a "ratings creep" over the past few years. In other words, a movie that would have been rated R before might now get by as a PG-13 film.

Marketing to Kids

The market sector made up of children and teenagers is a huge source of income for the entertainment industry. Today's young people have a lot of cash at their disposal, and a large portion of that money goes toward the purchase of video games, movie tickets, CDs, and DVDs. In addition, children and teens generally control what is on television throughout much of the day, and their wants and needs definitely influence how their families spend entertainment dollars. It's no wonder, then, that entertainment executives target their advertising to kids.

Selling stuff to children and young adults is good business, and there's nothing wrong or illegal about it in most cases. However, people do get upset when advertisers target the sale of harmful items such as cigarettes and alcohol to youngsters. The same holds true for violence. By agreeing to rate and label their products, the entertainment industry admits that some

The marketing hype surrounding some movies, videos games, recordings, and television shows attracts people of all ages—even those for whom the content may be inappropriate.

content may not be suitable for all audiences. Still, as a Federal Trade Commission report from 2000 showed, the industry continues to market to children as if the ratings didn't matter. The report revealed that 80 percent of R-rated movies, 70 percent of video games rated "M" or higher, and a full 100 percent of music recordings with "explicit content" warning labels were being marketed to those under the age of seventeen.

Marketing tactics include:

- Running commercials for adult products in the middle of kids' television programs
- Placing ads for restricted video games in magazines that teens read
- Arranging for pop-up ads on Internet sites that kids visit
- Showing trailers for R-rated movies before the screening of G-rated films

Legislating Violence in Entertainment

Over the years, politicians have attempted to control violent media content through legislation, or laws. These efforts have rarely gotten very far because First Amendment protections make it illegal for the government to pass laws that censor any person, group, or industry. Consequently, government officials have turned to more indirect ways of limiting violent content in the media.

Sometimes, these tactics make an impression on the entertainment media, like when Senate committee hearings convinced the Recording Industry Association of America to use parental warning labels on CDs. Other times, the results have been less impressive. Then there is the V-chip, which anti-violence crusaders might consider a victory and a defeat at the same time.

V-Chip

The government cannot legally dictate the content of television programs. So, politicians and the FCC have tried to find ways to

let viewers take matters into their own hands. The V-chip is one of their solutions. Mandated by Congress in 1996, the V-chip is a feature on television sets that lets viewers block programs based on their rating. Viewers decide which types of programs they want to block, and they set their V-chip accordingly. Once it is set, the chip picks up the coded rating of broadcast signals, which the networks and cable executives voluntarily have agreed to place on all programs. The chip is then able to block all shows that have a rating that is unacceptable to the viewer. To activate and set a V-chip, you must have its password. Anyone who doesn't know the password has no control over what gets blocked.

The fact that the technology is required in television sets is the victory part of this story. The outcome of the plan, however, is something of a defeat for industry watchdogs. V-chips are very effective when used properly, but studies have shown that most people either are not familiar with how to operate them, or they just don't bother to use them.

What You Can Do

Fortunately, we consumers don't need to depend on politicians or laws to do something about violence in the media. We can make a difference on our own. The people who produce violent media claim they are simply expressing themselves, which is probably true. But if you are tired of all the violent content in movies, music, television, and other entertainment media, you have the right to express yourself as well. Two ways you can do that are through boycotts and letter writing campaigns.

A boycott is a form of protest in which you refuse to buy a product or take part in an event. If you refuse to buy violent video games, attend violent movies, watch violent television shows,

or listen to radio stations that play violent music, you are boycotting these media. Boycotts work best when large groups of consumers participate, so it's important to involve your friends, neighbors, classmates, and anyone else you can think of who feels the same way that you do.

Letter writing campaigns also make a greater impact when many people are involved. To make it easier for large groups to participate, you might first create a template, or a basic outline, of your letter. In it, you can spell out your main objections about violent content and the steps you'd like to see taken to fix the situation. Others can add to the letter, if they want, or they can simply sign the sample letter and mail it. Targets of your campaign should be the companies that produce violent media; local, state, and federal government officials; and newspapers, where your thoughts can appear as a letter to the editor.

Remember, even if it's just you boycotting or writing letters, you're still having an effect. Every dollar you don't spend on violent entertainment and every word you put down on paper counts. Plus, you'll have the satisfaction of knowing that you stood up for what you believe.

Become an Informed Consumer

Don't buy a video game just because every one of your friends owns it. Try not to watch television shows you don't like only so you can talk about them the next day at school. In other words, really think about what you consume, meaning what you purchase or use.

A media literacy movement has started to pick up steam in the past few years. Media literacy requires consumers to change how they think about entertainment media. Media-literate

Violence in Movies, Music, and the Media

Questions for the Critic in You

- Why is the violent content included? Does it have any value other than to give me a thrill or to gross me out?

- How is the violence presented? Is it realistic or fantasy violence? Is it serious or played for laughs?

- Is the violence gratuitous, or does it help the film, television show, or song make a point?

- Are there any consequences to the violence, or do the villains literally get away with murder?

- Have I seen/heard this type of violence before in the media? If so, how did I feel while experiencing it and afterward? Good? Bad? Hyper? Angry?

Being choosy about what you consume is a good way to control the effect of violence in entertainment media.

consumers are not passive when they are being entertained. Instead, they think and act like critics. Think, for example, of how movie critics examine how films are put together—the acting, editing, plot, characters, and special effects—to determine if they are worth seeing. Be your own critic when it comes to violent media. See all the different parts that make up the whole, and figure out if those elements are included to thrill you, have the story make sense, or simply make a sale. Only then can you decide if the product you're consuming is worth your time.

Finding Balance

You don't have to give up all entertainment media to avoid violence. By doing a little research, you can find ways to amuse yourself that either aren't violent or have what you think is an acceptable amount of violent content. Another option would be to try what the media themselves do and self-regulate. Limit the number of hours you spend exposed to violent content. Or, find a tradeoff. Say that for every violent video game you play, you will spend half an hour reading a book. Balancing violent content with nonviolent content doesn't make you too cautious. It means you've become smarter about the way you choose to entertain yourself.

GLOSSARY

aggression Forceful action intended to dominate or hurt.

boycott The act of refusing to buy a product or take part in an event based on one's personal beliefs.

censorship Suppressing or changing the content of a song, television show, or movie.

congressional hearings Debates and presentations before the U.S. Congress that are designed to help the government decide whether it should take action by creating or enforcing laws.

console Cabinet holding the screen and controls for a video game.

correlation Relation or direct association between two things.

corridos Mexican ballads, often about violent historical events.

curb To restrain, check, or control.

delinquency Committing an offense or crime.

desensitization Process in which one takes in so much media violence that he or she becomes indifferent to all kinds of violence.

differentiate To separate or recognize a difference.

dopamine Chemical in the brain that makes us feel pleasure.

explicit Leaving no question as to meaning or intent.

Federal Communications Commission (FCC) U.S. government agency formed in 1934 to oversee radio and television broadcasting.

filtering Taking material that might be offensive out of the media.

First Amendment Addition to the U.S. Constitution that guarantees the right to free speech.

genre Type, or category.

glorify To elevate or cause to seem better than the actual condition.

gratuitous violence Violent content that appears in the media without any reason for it.

gruesome Repulsive, horrible.

habituation Process of becoming so used to media violence that it doesn't bother one anymore.

mainframe Large, fast computer.

media literacy Thinking and acting like a media critic.

new media Forms of electronic communication made possible by computers.

objectionable Offensive.

physiological Having to do with the body.

potent Powerful, forceful.

realism Style of media in which the violent action in media is as close to genuine as possible.

sacrilegious Against religious beliefs.

self-regulation When the media set up guidelines governing their own industries.

unabated At full force.

V-chip Technology installed in television sets that lets viewers block programs based on their rating.

FOR MORE INFORMATION

Canadians Concerned About Violence in Entertainment (C-CAVE)
167 Glen Road
Toronto, ON M4W 2W8
Canada
Web site: http://www.c-cave.com
C-CAVE is a national nonprofit that holds conferences, workshops, and public meetings, and provides referrals and resources on violence and entertainment.

Center for Media Literacy
4727 Wilshire Boulevard, Suite 403
Los Angeles, CA 90010
(213) 913-4177
Web site: http://www.medialit.org
The Center for Media Literacy provides media literacy materials and information.

The Dove Foundation
535 East Fulton, Suite 1A
Grand Rapids, MI 49503
(616) 454-5021
Web site: http://www.dove.org
This nonprofit organization promotes family-friendly entertainment. It provides movie reviews, marketing resources for film producers, and a film festival.

Media Awareness Network
1500 Merivale Road, 3rd Floor
Ottawa, ON K2E 6Z5
Canada
(613) 224-7721
(800) 896-3342

Web site: http://www.media-awareness.ca/english
The Media Awareness Network provides literary and database resources
that help people understand how the media work and affect lifestyle choices.

Media Scope
12711 Ventura Boulevard
Studio City, CA 01694
(818) 508-2080
Media Scope promotes positive social issues in media; it's also a clearinghouse
for media violence materials.

Web Sites

Due to the changing nature of Internet links, Rosen Publishing
has developed an online list of Web sites related to the subject
of this book. This site is updated regularly. Please use this link
to access the list:

http://www.rosenlinks.com/vas/vmmm

Cefrey, Holly. *Coping with Media Violence*. New York, NY: Rosen Publishing Group, 2001.

Gerdes, Louise I., ed. *Opposing Viewpoints: Media Violence*. Farmington Hills, MI: Greenhaven Press, 2003.

Haugen, David M., ed. *Is Media Violence a Problem?* Farmington Hills, MI: Greenhaven Press, 2006.

Jones, Gerard. *Killing Monsters: Why Children Need Fantasy, Super Heroes, and Make-Believe Violence*. New York, NY: Basic Books (Perseus Books Group), 2002.

Kamalipour, Yahya R. *Media, Sex, Violence, and Drugs in the Global Village*. Lanham, MD: Rowman and Littlefield Publishers, Inc., 2001.

Potter, W. James. *The 11 Myths About Media Violence*. Thousand Oaks, CA: Sage Publications, Inc., 2003.

Strasburger, Victor C., and Barbara Wilson. *Children, Adolescents, and the Media*. Thousand Oaks, CA: Sage Publications, Inc., 2002.

Torr, James D. *Violence in the Media*. Farmington Hills, MI: Greenhaven Press, 2000.

American Psychological Association. "Violence in the Media: Psychologists Help Protect Children from Harmful Effects." APA Online, Psychology Matters. February 19, 2004. Retrieved September 20, 2007 (www.psychologymatters. org/mediaviolence.html).

Anderson, Craig A. "Violent Video Games: Myths, Facts, and Unanswered Questions." *Psychological Science Agenda (APA)*, Volume 16, No. 5, October 2003.

Ash, Rebecca L. "The Payne Fund Studies." Angelfire.com. March 1999. Retrieved October 2007 (http://www.angelfire. com/journal/worldtour99/paynefund.html).

Bjorkvist, Kaj. "Sex Differences in Physical, Verbal, and Indirect Aggression: A Review of Recent Research." *Sex Roles: A Journal of Research*, February 1994. Retrieved October 2007 (http://findarticles.com/p/articles/mi_m2294/is_n3-4_v30/ ai_15383471).

Brick, Michael. "Rap Takes Center Stage at Trial in Killing of Two Detectives." *New York Times*, Vol. 156, Issue 53791, December 12, 2006, pp. B1–B2.

Centerwall, Brandon S. "Our Cultural Perplexities: Television and Violent Crime." *Public Interest*, Spring 1993, Issue 111, pp. 56–71.

Cocks, Jay. "Rock Is a Four-Letter Word." *Time*, September 30, 1985, Vol. 126, Issue 13, p. 70.

Common Sense Media.com. "FCC Report Urges Limits on TV Violence." April 26, 2007. Retrieved September 20, 2007 (www.commonsensemedia.org/resources/violence. php?id=14).

Dirks, Tim. "The Great Train Robbery: A Review." Filmsite.org. Retrieved October 2007 (http://www.filmsite.org/grea.html).

Ewing, Tom. "Adverse Effects of Violent Media Imagery on Young People." February 2005. Retrieved November 2007 (www.medpagetoday.com/PublicHealthPolicy/HealthPolicy/tbl/526).

Farhi, Paul, and Frank Aherns. "FCC Seeks to Rein in Violent Shows." *Washington Post*, April 24, 2007, p. C01.

Funk, Jeanne B., et. al. "Violence Exposure in Real-Life, Video Games, Television, Movies, and the Internet: Is There Desensitization?" *Journal of Adolescence*, Vol. 27, 2004, pp. 23–39.

Heins, Marjorie, and Christina Cho. "Media Literacy: An Alternative to Censorship." *The Free Expression Policy Project*, Fall 2003. Retrieved November 2007 (http://www.fepproject.org/policyreports/medialiteracy.html).

Hoerrner, Keisha L. "The Forgotten Battles: Congressional Hearings on Television Violence in the 1950s." *The Web Journal of Mass Communications Research*, June 1999. Retrieved November 2007 (www.scripps.ohiou.edu/wjmcr/vol02/2-3a-B.htm).

Huesmann, L. R., J. Moise-Titus, C. Podolski, and L. D. Eron. "Longitudinal Relations Between Children's Exposure to TV Violence and their Aggressive and Violent Behavior in Young Adulthood: 1977–1992." *Developmental Psychology*, Vol. 39, 2003, pp. 201–221.

Jackson, Peter. "The History of the Internet." *IT Week*. Retrieved November 2007 (http://www.itweek.co.uk/personal-computer-world/features/2170093/feature-history-internet).

Jenkins, Lucille, et al. "An Evaluation of the Motion Picture Association of America's Treatment of Violence in PG-, PG-13-, and R-Rated Films." *Pediatrics: Official Journal of the*

American Academy of Pediatrics, Vol. 115, Issue 5, May 2005, pp. e512–e517.

Jowett, Garth S. "'A Capacity for Evil': The 1915 Supreme Court Mutual Decision." In *Controlling Hollywood: Censorship and Regulation in the Studio Era*. Piscataway, NJ: Rutgers University Press, 1999.

Kirsh, Steven J. *Children, Adolescents, and Media Violence: A Critical Look at the Research*. Thousand Oaks, CA: Sage Publications, Inc., 2006.

Leymarie, Isabelle. "Rock 'n' Revolt: Violence in Music." *UNESCO Courier*, February 1993. Retrieved November 4, 2007 (http://findarticles.com/p/articles/mi_m1310/is_1993_Feb/ai_13574218).

Media Awareness Network. "The Business of Media Violence." Retrieved November 2007 (http://www.media-awareness.ca/english/issues/violence/business_media_violence.cfm).

Media Awareness Network. "Violent and Hateful Content." Retrieved November 2007 (http://www.bewebaware.ca/english/violent.aspx).

MediaKnowAll. "The Representation of Violence in the Media." Retrieved October 2007 (http://www.mediaknowall.com/violence/representviol.html).

Newton, John. "PG-13 = Not Safe for Kids." *AgoraVox*. Retrieved November 2007 (http://www.agoravox.com/article.php3?id_article=6205).

Queensland University of Technology. "Computer Games: Brief History of Violence in Computer Games." *M/Cyclopedia of New Media*. October 2004. Retrieved November 2007 (http://wiki.media-culture.org.au/index.php/Computer_Games_-_Brief_History_of_Violence_in_Computer_Games).

Schecter, Harold. *Savage Pastimes*. New York, NY: St. Martin's Press, 2005.

Signorelli, Nancy. "Prime-Time Violence 1993–2001: Has the Picture Really Changed?" *Journal of Broadcasting & Electronic Media*, March 3, 2003, pp. 36–61.

Smith, Craig R. "Violence & Media: Overview." First Amendment Center. May 2007. Retrieved November 2007 (http://www.firstamendmentcenter.org/speech/arts/topic.aspx?topic=violence_media).

Sparks, Glenn G. "Violence in the Media, History of Research On." *Encyclopedia of Communication and Information*. Retrieved October 2007 (http://www.bookrags.com/research/violence-in-the-media-history-of-re-eci-03).

About the Author

Jeanne Nagle is a journalist, writer, and editor living in upstate New York. Other titles she has written for Rosen Publishing include *Drug Addiction*, *Polysubstance Abuse*, and *Marijuana*. Her lifelong fascination with and affection for entertainment media has been heightened through research for this book.

Photo Credits

Cover © MGM/courtesy Everett Collection; cover (right), p. 16 © AFP/Getty Images; cover (background) © www.istockphoto.com/Marcela Barsse; back cover © www.istockphoto.com/Gordon Poropat; p. 1 © www.istockphoto.com; p. 4 © HBO/The Everett Collection; pp. 8, 10, 14 © Photofest; p. 12 © Time-Life Pictures/Getty Images; pp. 18, 27, 34 © AP Photos; pp. 22, 24, 48 © Getty Images; p. 39 Shutterstock; p. 43 © epa/Corbis; p. 44 © FilmMagic/Getty Images; p. 46 © David Young-Wolff/ Photo Edit; p. 52 © www.istockphoto.com/ Owen Price.

Designer: Nelson Sa; **Editor:** Christopher Roberts
Photo Researcher: Marty Levick